I0463230

Money-Makin' Mama

How to Generate a Steady Income as a Stay-at-Home Mom

by Amber N. Carter

Table of Contents

My Story (Preface)

As I was typing away in my cubicle at work, all I could think about was meeting my precious baby girl in only 15 weeks. I had waited so long for this baby; many times babies aren't exactly in the plans, but for my husband and myself, it was something we'd been looking forward to for years.

Over the past few months, I had thoroughly mastered the art of processing paperwork and looking busy while concentrating on something totally separate (my Jada, of course). As the days slowly ticked by, however, my anxiety rose along with my excited anticipation. "How are we going to possibly afford for me to stay at home? I can't fathom working full-time and dropping my daughter off at day care. I want, more than anything, to stay home with her. How am I going to feel when I stop working? Will I have enough adult interaction? Is it the right time to start my own business?" All of these thoughts constantly flooded through my mind – as if I needed something in addition to the excess of hormones already flowing through me.

I prayed and prayed. I wanted to stay at home with my baby; I just didn't see how the numbers were going to work out, practically. I needed a miracle. Starting my own business had always been a dream for me. I grew up with my mom at home and my dad working from home; he owned (and still owns) a plumbing business. I wanted to give my kids the same gift I had been given – a mommy at home.

Even though I didn't quite know what my business would morph into and with absolutely no clients lined up, I registered my business on September 4, 2008 (15 weeks before Jada was born). I didn't actively search for clients; I just prayed. And waited. And waited.

Jada was born December 20, 2008 (I went into labor 12 hours after my last scheduled day of work... I'm so proud of my punctual girl!). Still no clients. A week went by. Still no clients, but I wasn't worried. When Jada was 9 days old, my friend, Kalen, stopped by my house to visit. In the midst of our conversation, she asked me about my work plans. I told her that I was going to resign from my full-time federal career once my sick and vacation days were depleted and *start up a bookkeeping business so that I could stay home with Jada. Get ready for the miracle… Kalen's close friend, Lisa, was currently looking for a bookkeeper. What a blessing. I gave Kalen my card and within a week, I met Lisa and started working from home.*

Since then, I've accumulated 9 additional clients and my business is growing at the perfect rate. I'm able to raise my daughter at home and run the business I've always dreamed of. As I'm writing this, I'm actually anticipating the arrival of our baby boy; he's expected to make his appearance in about 10 weeks. Although I realize my life will, once again, change forever, I'm eagerly anticipating this exciting new addition to our family. My business model is in the process of being tweaked, in order to allow me to work fewer hours and to generate a more lucrative passive income.

Because I feel so blessed to have this life, I want to share what I've learned over the past couple of years with other moms. This isn't just meant for the full-time working mom who deeply desires to be at home with her children (although I most relate to you!), but it is also meant for mommies in the following situations:

1. The mom who is already at home with her children, but is either wanting or needing to earn some extra money.
2. The mom who is happy to be at home, but wishes she had some other outlet (social interaction, creative or artistic outlet, physical activity, or other forms of productivity).
3. The mom who already has a home business, but it's not quite working out the way that she planned.

This guide will educate, encourage and equip stay-at-home moms to successfully start up and happily maintain a business without sacrificing time with her family. The following questions will be specifically addressed:

1. What type of a business should I start?
2. How can I find the time to work? What will I do with my kids while I'm working?
3. Can I provide health insurance for my family and myself?
4. Is it possible to contribute to a retirement fund?
5. What if I don't want to start a business, but I still need to earn some extra money?
6. How do other moms do it?

At first, we'll discuss the questions that you should ask yourself before even starting up your business. After that, we'll discuss the all-important topics of finances, time-management, very affordable ways to occupy your children while you work, retirement and insurance options, and what type of business you should start. All throughout this guide, you will find stories of moms who have once been in your position, but have all found success in various ways and who would love to share their wisdom with you.

This guide is meant to supplement the entrepreneurial guide, The Free Agent Formula, which outlines techniques for generating customers, increasing revenue, and finding new income streams. Therefore, I won't be diving into those topics. I will, however, explain, in detail, topics that stay-at-home moms face and recommendations for how to conquer those challenges.

Let's get started!

Does your husband/family support your idea?

Before you go out and register your business, I would strongly recommend sketching out a rough business plan. Figure out how much money you'd like to make, how you're planning on earning it, what you're going to do with the children (even if your plan is to work while they're sleeping – just write that down), and what sort of a time commitment you're looking at. If you're married, sit down with your husband and share your ideas. Warning – I am about to say something very stereotypical, but am going to say it anyway - Men tend to be very concrete thinkers. He's going to want solutions to potential problems. He'll want hard figures and a concrete plan. Give it to him. Really think about possible roadblocks and try to come up with solutions before you even bring it up to him. Explain to him why you want to do this, how it's possible, and how the kids will be affected. Show him how you really can develop the extra income without compromising your family.

He may love your idea. He may hate it. He may have some ideas that would make it even better. Listen to him. If starting a business would somehow add strain to your marriage, then don't do it. It's not worth it. After all, if you're starting the business to help your family and it winds up causing disagreement and hurting your marriage, are you really accomplishing your goal?

If you're not married, I would recommend discussing your business plan with a close member of your family or a close friend. It's important that you have support during the transition of starting up a new venture.

If you don't have an intricate business model already completed, that's okay. That's actually fantastic. I have personally found that my best ideas and concrete plans come when I'm feeling a bit lost. With that it mind, let's consider other questions that you should ask yourself before starting a business.

Why Do You Want to Work from Home?

- So that you can quit your job outside the home?
- You can't imagine leaving your newborn 10 hours each day, 5 days each week?
- You enjoy working, just not at the expense of your family?

ALL MATERIALS COPYRIGHT ©2011 AMBER N. CARTER

- To supplement your husband's income?
- To buy those new, funky shoes without feeling guilty for spending your husband's hard-earned money?
- To set aside money for something exciting – like the vacation you've always dreamed about?
- To utilize your college degree?
- To have a social outlet or adult time?
- To start a retirement fund? (That's right! A stay-at-home mom CAN contribute to a retirement fund! We'll talk about that in more detail later.)

Keep your goals in mind when you're creating your business plan. Let's be realistic; when you're a mom, you don't have a lot of "free time". If your "free time" is spent working, don't you want to spend that time doing something you absolutely love?

Because many traditional business models recommend the old fashioned (and very expensive) way of starting a business, which includes taking out huge loans and placing financial risks on your personal assets, I would not recommend following those models. If your goal is to create a steady income stream without much risk, then why would you want to put yourself and your family in that position? For those reasons, I would strongly recommend following the *Free Agent Formula*, which is all about new ways to advertise and be successful with no to very little risk.

What's Your Personal/Business Goal?

There's a reason why this isn't two separate questions - when you're working from home, it's difficult to keep your personal life and business life separate.

Because it's so easy for me to want more for my business and desire more time to work, it's important for me to keep my priorities in perspective. I admit that I struggle with my priorities at times. What I need to remember is that I chose to quit my full-time job so that I could stay at home with my kids. Sure, I have an income goal that I set every month and it's important that I meet that goal. However, I have a tendency to want to work and earn more than I need to, which could easily cause me to sacrifice my family time. I enjoy running my business, but I need to keep my primary goal of being a stay-at-home mom a top priority. This might mean that I will turn down job opportunities that sound like fun or that I will intentionally not pick up an extra project because it would mean that I would have to sit my daughter in front of a video all afternoon. Those are all personal boundaries that I've set for myself. Your goals may be different and that's fine. Just make sure that you stick to your goals and remember why you chose to do what you're doing.

How much do you NEED to earn?

This practical question is obviously important to consider when planning your business. Some moms just want an opportunity to earn some extra spending money. Others have to earn a certain monthly amount just to pay the bills. Make sure that you carefully calculate your overhead costs and estimated expenses and subtract that from your gross profit to figure out your actual net income. For example, if you figure that you can earn a specific amount each month from your services, but you'll have to pay for a website, some computer upgrades, & office supplies, make sure that you factor those costs into your calculation.

When you're determining how much money you need to earn to stay at home, remember that you'll be saving money in many areas by not working outside of the home. The obvious expense would be childcare costs and the cost of commuting, but don't forget about the daily savings. For example, you will be more likely to make dinner at home rather than picking up take-out on the way home from work. You won't have to purchase as many work clothes (you may want a couple of nice outfits for when you meet clients in person, but you most likely won't need to wear a business suit five days per week). You won't have to donate money to Secretary's Day, a co-worker's birthday present or retirement party AND you won't have to pick up that fruit platter for the occasional potluck anymore. Those expenses can really add up.

How can you easily factor in all of those variables? Below, you'll find a Sample Worksheet. I listed the expenses as a running tab so that you can see your paycheck slowly dwindle away, one expense at a time. Your costs will probably be a little different and you may even have some additional costs that aren't even on this worksheet. I'm not including health insurance premiums, in this example, but that should also be factored in if

SECTION 1 – Questions You Should Ask Yourself

you provide those benefits for your family. You may want to keep a little tab, over the next month, of everything you're paying for because you're working outside of the home just to make sure you're factoring in all of the necessary variables.

SAMPLE WORKSHEET

How Much Are You Really Earning?
(Based on an annual salary of $45,000 and tax filing status of Married Filing Jointly)

Monthly Gross Income	**$3,750**
Tithe or Charitable Contributions	-$375
Federal Taxes (15%)	-$563
State Taxes (varies; example is 5%)	-$188
Social Security Taxes (7.65%)	-$286
Net Monthly Income (Your Paycheck Amount)	$2,338
Cost-of-Work Expenses	
Child Care	-$750
Transportation (gas $, etc.)	-$110
Meals/Coffee/Snacks ($5/day average)	-$100
Takeout Dinners	-$200
Work Clothes	-$150
Hair/Nails	-$75
Parking at Work	-$25
Dry Cleaning (for work clothes)	-$35
Miscellaneous Gifts for Co-Workers	-$10
Kid's hot lunches instead of sack lunches	-$30
Actual, Spendable Income at the End of the Month	**$853**

In this example, even though you're earning $45,000 each year, you're really only left with about $850 each month. Is that worth your lifestyle? Or better yet, **could you make that much money from home**? No, money that you earn at home isn't tax free (you'll still have to pay taxes), but you don't have to pay taxes on ALL of it, like you do when you're an employee for someone else. In fact, if you're working from home, you can even subtract the cost of expenses you're already paying (like a part of your

SECTION 1 – Questions You Should Ask Yourself

rent or mortgage!). For more detailed information on this tax stuff, skip down a few pages to Section 5 "Speaking of Money".

Does your bottom line ($853 in this example) look a little daunting? Don't forget that even if you can't EARN that amount, maybe a combination of EARNING and SAVING could bring you to that goal.

Money-saving tip:
Many attorneys offer free or low-cost consultations! Don't pay more than you have to for legal advice!

Think about this for a second – which is better? Saving $100 by frugal spending or earning $100? Saving $100 gives you an extra $100 in your pocket, right? How about earning $100... does that give you $100 in your pocket? Not really. After taxes, it'll probably be about $75. Now which one is better?

Here are some practical money-saving tips that you could consider:

- Pack school lunches instead of purchasing hot lunches
- Cut your family's hair instead of paying for haircuts
- Carry healthy snacks in the car (instead of stopping by fast food)
- Price shop for Dry Cleaning services (is someone else cheaper?)
- Cut back on Starbucks (I invested in my own espresso machine & broke-even in about 2 months!)
- Cut the cable bill
- Shop around for telephone/internet services – are you paying the lowest amount?
- Shop clearance racks or second-hand stores for clothing
- Check out "Cultural Passes" at your local library (free admission to local entertainment spots) instead of paying admission fees for entertainment.
- Turn off lights when you're not in the room
- Take short showers instead of baths
- In the winter, leave the oven open after baking, while it's cooling down, to heat up the house (when children are out of the kitchen, obviously). In the summer, avoid using the oven – use a crockpot & plug it in outside instead of in the kitchen, so it won't heat up the house!

- Wash laundry in cold water instead of warm or hot water
- Shop around for the best auto and homeowner's insurance & switch, if necessary.
- Make sure you have the lowest possible mortgage interest rate
- Buy used instead of new
- Whenever you purchase something online, check to see if there's a coupon code somewhere out there to give you a larger discount at checkout (www.currentcodes.com is a good site, among many, to check).
- USE COUPONS (my favorite couponing/money-saving blogs are www.moneysavingmom.com, www.frugallivingnw.com, and www.commonsensewithmoney.com)

Do You Actually WANT to Start a Business?

Starting a business is like having another child. There are schedules to work around, messes to clean up, and frequent feedings (think time commitment). There are also certain personal qualifications that are necessary for just about any profession that you want to run from home. They are as follows: self-motivation, excellent time management skills, basic organization skills, and the ability to make decisions, focus, and work independently. It is a big responsibility. Make sure it's something you really WANT to do before you dive in.

Maybe you actually just want to set some boundaries instead of starting a business. I have a friend who has an incredible knack for party planning. Because she found herself planning parties for friends in every second of her valuable spare time, she just assumed that she should start a party planning business. After discussing how she felt about how she was spending her time, we discovered that she didn't actually want to start a business, she just wanted to be able to charge for her time and services without feeling guilty.

All she needed was to set some boundaries. She decided to simply order some business cards and type up a price sheet. That way, when somebody asked her if she could plan an upcoming party, she could politely say, "I'd love to! Here's my business card and a price sheet. Take a look at the options that I offer and give me a call, if you're interested". Problem solved.

It's important to set professional boundaries immediately, otherwise, people might take advantage of your skill and just expect it as a free courtesy. You always have the option, of course, of working pro bono, but you shouldn't feel obligated to work for free just because you have a relationship with the client.

Disclaimer: Please make sure that you follow the legal regulations in your area. You may be required to attain a business license or register with your state. For detailed checklists regarding this area, check out the "Ready To Launch" guide for the *Free Agent Formula* and consult a local business attorney.

What's Your Passion?

- People?
- Creative Expression?
- Productivity?
- Physical Activity?

Transform your hobby into an income opportunity. Maybe you love training for marathons, but you wish that you could have a running buddy on those 4-hour runs. Do you like teaching others? How about starting a marathon coaching business? Wouldn't those 20 miles be even more fun if you earned $50 (or $100 or whatever you decide to charge) in the process? Not to mention, you could broaden your circle of friends who also enjoy running. Sounds like a win-win situation to me!

Maybe you're one of those amazingly crafty individuals. I have a friend who hadn't sewn a pillow in her entire life, but after her son was born and she stayed at home and decided to pick up sewing. She's now creating custom-tailored tuxedos for babies. What a fun opportunity to earn some cash!

It is vital for you to be passionate about your business. If you're earning money doing something that you hate, then what's the point?

When I was pregnant with Jada, I constantly held mini brainstorming sessions with myself (Wonder how I spent my 10-min. breaks at work? Here's your answer.) I made a list of activities I enjoyed and found that I naturally excelled. It looked something like this:

SECTION 1 – Questions You Should Ask Yourself

- Organizing stuff
- Numbers
- Helping others
- Research & writing
- Detailed projects

What type of a business could best utilize those traits? Bookkeeping! Not only could I practically use my natural gifts, but this type of service-based business also requires very low overhead costs (pretty much none since I work in my home) and extremely flexible hours (vital while simultaneously caring for a newborn).

Melissa Berry (www.missionarychocolates.com) has a passion for helping others lead a healthy life. She Is an incredible single mom to her son Elijah, a practicing Naturopathic Doctor, and the owner of Missionary Chocolates, a vegan truffle company, in Portland Oregon. Not only is she passionate about her work, you could say she's on a mission.

Melissa's Story

I'm on a mission to change the paradigm of health care.

Mom to:
Elijah
Passion:
Helping Others Lead a Healthy Life
Money-Makin' Opportunity:
Naturopathic Doctor and
Chocolatier

It was November 2007. I was a single mom to my amazing 16-month-old son, Elijah, and a full-time student at NCNM (National College of Natural Medicine). I had just completed my exams and Christmas was quickly approaching. I wanted to give something special to my mom for Christmas.

My mom loves chocolate, however, she's a vegan. Honestly, at that time, there were no good vegan chocolates. She always complained that they were grainy and bitter. How perfect would it be if I could make her delicious vegan chocolates for Christmas? I decided to check out a few books from the local library just to learn a bit more about chocolate. I quickly discovered that the chemistry of chocolate is pretty intense; I began to study the art of chocolate like I studied for my boards. After spending 2 weeks straight trying various forms of dairy substitutes (rice milk, soy milk, you name it!), I discovered coconut milk. Ahh, that's what I was looking for. For Christmas, I presented her with a large selection of delicious, vegan truffles. She loved them. In fact, she enjoyed them so much that she shared them with her friends! They loved them too. It was then that I decided to start a business. In only two months, Missionary Chocolates was registered with the state and an official business. I started creating my delectable truffles in my own kitchen when my son was sleeping and would sell them at the local Farmer's Market. That whole spring, I could be found on various days of the week manning my table at the Farmer's Market with a text book in hand, studying for my boards, while simultaneously watching my son crawl around a blanket and playing with toys.

ALL MATERIALS COPYRIGHT ©2011 AMBER N. CARTER

In September 2008, I decided to enter the Northwest Chocolate Festival just to network with other business owners and market my product. I showed up with my purple tablecloth and little silver platter of lemon truffles and started sharing my product. When the award ceremony was wrapping up, I heard the third place winner announced followed by the second. I was about to walk over to the refreshments when, all of a sudden, I heard the first place announcement – "Melissa Berry with Missionary Chocolates". I was shocked and honored to win first place at the Northwest Chocolate Festival among over 30 larger, more established chocolatiers.

My business has been a constant whirlwind of excitement and recognition. My sister, Vanessa Holden, joined me shortly after the Northwest Chocolate Festival and is now my Marketing and Sales Director. We have won four awards for our truffles, which are now sold in three states- Oregon, California, and New York (in addition to online sales). We quickly established relationships with local farmers in order to establish a sustainable supply of local ingredients. In fact, our furthest ingredient is from Tualatin, Oregon, which is only 20 miles away. Up until two months ago, I was handcrafting chocolates in my personal kitchen. I'm proud to report that we now have a production facility just a few blocks from my home. We specialize in custom orders; I love combining my scientific knowledge with my creative passion to create truffles for customers with a variety of dietary restrictions.

You may be wondering where the name "Missionary Chocolates" came from. I have a desire to help others, especially those who are chronically ill or cancer patients. One day, I would love to create a new model for medicine by establishing a hospital that's more like a holistic healing center. It will provide not only a more integrated approach for treatment options for those who truly need medical attention, but an incredible opportunity for ND (naturopathic) students to utilize their skills with clinical hours in their last year of school. This also provides an affordable and sustainable model considering the students' clinical hours are unpaid! I'm on a mission to change the paradigm of health care.

I feel that I'm living the dream. I have a beautiful son whom I have the privilege of raising, a business that offers a delicious *product that anyone with almost any dietary restriction can enjoy, the opportunity to utilize my medical training (yes, I am also a practicing Naturopathic Doctor) and a goal to change the history of medical care.*

I would encourage any mom with the desire to start her own business to just do it. You can do anything you put your mind to. In fact, if you're feeling a little scared, you're probably doing the right thing.

ALL MATERIALS COPYRIGHT ©2011 AMBER N. CARTER

SECTION 1 – Questions You Should Ask Yourself

How Do You Like to Work?

Do you prefer to work independently or as part of a team?

I've been asked before if I'm a "team player". My typical answer is, "Yes, in the Cross-Country sense of the word." If you have no idea what I'm talking about, this explanation should help. In a cross-country race, the first person to cross the finish line is given one point. The second person is given two points. The 55th person is given 55 points. You get the point (pun intended). Anyway, the top five runners on each team total their points and that is the team score. The team with the lowest score wins. Every player runs his or her own race, yet each member of the team also relies on the success of his or her teammates.

I love completing the race on my own, but I equally love enjoying a victory with the entire team. Keeping that in mind, I designed a business model, which allows me to work on my own, yet also creates opportunities for me to celebrate. Specifically, I find great enjoyment from organizing paperwork and financial statements for my clients. I equally enjoy getting to know them as individuals and celebrating business successes with them.

Make sure that your business plan accommodates the way in which you enjoy working. If you tend to be lonely, try to build in ways to spend time with others. Even though I work by myself in my living room while my daughter is sleeping, I'm constantly on the phone with clients and connecting with other small business owners; this social interaction is important to me. For specific tips on how to work for yourself, but not by yourself, check out the "Free Thoughts" CD that's included with the *Free Agent Formula* package.

What's Your Personality?

There are many good personality tests out there. One that I particularly appreciate is the Myers Briggs Type Indicator. After answering a series of questions, this test reveals specific ways the test-taker perceives the world and makes decisions. Even if you think you know yourself pretty well, it's helpful to be given definitions for the way you interact with others, process information, and make decisions. These definitions can help you cater your business plan to best suit your personality. Not to mention, it could also help you identify personality traits of people you'd like to work with.

My Myers Briggs personality type is ESTJ (extraverted, sensing, thinking, & judging). In a nutshell, that means that I receive energy from people (extraverted), I'm more likely to trust concrete facts than I am intuition (sensing), I prefer to make decisions based on what I think rather than what I feel (thinking), and I would rather plan activities in advance rather than be spontaneous (judging). All of these qualities directly influence how I conduct business; they also make me more aware of my areas of weakness (or should I say - potential growth?). For example, because I prefer to plan my activities ahead of time, it's easy for me to become overwhelmed if all of my plans change at the last minute. Therefore, I've decided to always schedule in some "free time" into my schedule so that if someone needs a task completed at an unexpected time or a friend wants to spend time with me at the last minute, I have that time available.

Just because I enjoy bookkeeping, doesn't mean that everyone else would be content and succeed in bookkeeping. The "STJ" part of my personality thrives in this career. Because I work by myself at home, I have to get creative with the "E" part of my personality. I thrive on interacting with others and taking leadership in situations. Public speaking gives me a crazy high. Attending a conference where I know absolutely nobody is thrilling and I love introducing myself to potential clients. Therefore, I intentionally schedule in those opportunities for myself.

As I mentioned before, I've been running all aspects of my business for the past 2 years. Now that my second child is on the way, I realize that I still want to earn the same amount of (actually a little more) money than I am currently, yet my hours are going to become more limited. I want to remain the face of my business and primary contact for all of my clients. My only problem is that I won't have the ability to physically put in the hours required to keep up with all of these new clients.

My solution? Hire a handful of other Stay-at-Home Moms who would prefer to just be given the work and will accept a smaller payment (than what I am charging the clients) in return for not having the responsibility of finding the clients themselves. I can then enjoy being the face of my business while my contractors enjoy the freedom to work when they want to and without the pressure of answering phone calls from clients when their children are screaming in the background. My ideal Stay-at-Home contractor has the personality ISTJ (still very detail oriented and loves concrete facts and numbers), but doesn't necessarily want to go searching for new clients on her own (introverted).

When you're creating a business model, take into consideration your personality and the personality of others you would like to work with. I know I've said it before, but I just can't say it enough – if you're not passionate about your business and it's not working for you, then it's just not working. Take the opportunity now to create a business that will complement you and give you energy.

Do you have a specific skill set that sets you apart?

Are you known as the "technical expert" in a particular subject? Do your friends always ask you for help with fixing their computer, choosing a fun outfit, photographing their family, or planning a party? If you're the "go to" person in a particular area, that's usually a pretty good indication that you have a gift in that area – what a perfect place to start for a business idea!

My friend, Mindy (www.mindystrauss.com/life_photography/), decided to start a photography business because she was the "go to" person in her group of friends. Let's take a look at her story...

Mindy's Story

I love stylizing photo shoots and dreaming up creative ways to make each one unique and beautiful.

Mom to:
Hudson & Marlowe
Passion:
Making People Feel Beautiful & Special
Money-Makin' Opportunity:
Photographer

I have always loved photography and was encouraged by friends to start charging for my time. I prayed with my husband about it and decided to go for it. A big factor, in our decision, was the cost of equipment - photography is an expensive hobby. To move it beyond that point, I decided to develop it into a business and see what would happen. I wanted to develop something that I could continue (at whatever rate I felt comfortable) once we had children. I started my business approximately 3 years before my first child was born. My children are now 1 year old and 3 years old.

I honestly love my business - in many ways it doesn't really feel like one. I love stylizing photo shoots and dreaming up creative ways to make each one unique and beautiful. I love making gorgeous images for people... making them feel beautiful and special. My least favorite part of running my business is saying "no" to people, but my first priority is being a mom and a wife. Because I tend to be non-confrontational, I occasionally sacrifice my style and artistic perspective to please a client and I'm never happy with the results. I'm learning to speak up and not get bowled over. I think everyone ends up happier in the end.

My husband has a very flexible job so he can always watch our kids when I do a photo shoot, which I generally limit to 2-3 per month. For post processing and other tasks, I just squeeze in the hours when I can, but that's usually naptime or evenings when my husband has something going on. Creative shooting for my etsy site happens all the time - when I'm out with my family, etc... my camera is a near constant companion. The beauty of *websites like istockphoto.com, etsy.com, or zazzle.com (I use all of them) is that there is some initial work, but then they essentially work for you without requiring constant hours.*

One major challenge that I have while trying to juggle a business and raise my children at the same time is balance. It's easy for me to get excited and dreamy about what props I could get, studio space, and business concepts, so I need to keep my priorities in check. My priority is being a mommy and a wife so that always takes precedence over photography - I LOVE my role and wouldn't trade it for the most amazing studio and equipment in the world. There's just a balance there and keeping the passion focused is key.

Personally, I believe that a mother's role is to build up and nurture her family. If you're considering starting a business, I would urge you to really pray about the time given to the business... if you can do both well, then great! If one must suffer, then make sure it's not your family. Everyone has a gift - those are the easiest things to turn into a business. The Internet has a lot of avenues to use and build your ideas. It's definitely doable and really fun, so go for it!

Would you actually enjoy working at home?

If you enjoy physically going to work and would rather have someone else handle your tax withholdings and all that legal stuff, you may want to consider picking up a part-time job in the evenings or weekend (or whatever would work with your family's schedule). My friend, Kathleen stays at home full-time with her daughter during the day, but teaches English Composition one night each week at the local community college. Let's look at her story...

ALL MATERIALS COPYRIGHT ©2011 AMBER N. CARTER

Kathleen's Story

This job gives me the flexibility of working outside of the home for a few hours each week and the ability to set my own hours.

Mom to:
Cora
Passion:
Teaching & Public Speaking
Money-Makin' Opportunity:
Part-time English Professor

I 've always known that once I had kids, I would want to stay at home with them. With that in mind, I started teaching part-time at the local community college about a year and a half before my daughter was born; I was hoping to establish a relationship with them that would continue after I became a mom. It worked! My daughter is now two years old.

Teaching is a perfect fit to my personality. I'm an extrovert who enjoys public speaking. I'm more of a "big picture" person rather than a detail oriented one. I cringe at the thought of being a manager or supervisor. This job gives me flexibility of working outside of the home for a few hours each week and the ability to set my own hours. I know that if I stopped teaching, I would really miss it. I also love being able to use my college degree; I have a Masters Degree in Middle English Literature, and I teach English Composition.

Teaching part-time also works very well with my family's schedule. I teach one night each week. My husband arrives home from work at about 4:30pm, which is when I leave to go teach for a few hours. In that regard, I have fixed office hours. As for lesson planning and grading papers, however, I squeeze in the work when my daughter is napping.

Most of the time, my daughter's naptime gives me sufficient time to lesson plan and grade papers. During the times when it doesn't (such as when term papers are due), I swap play dates with a friend; we take turns watching each other's children so *that we can each take a turn working.*

The most challenging aspect of working and being a full-time mom, is the sacrifice of other responsibilities and my own personal time. Since I'm working while Cora's napping, it makes it difficult to work on other household duties. Fixing dinner, cleaning the house, paying bills, or just my own personal time has to be a second priority. That can definitely become difficult.

If you're considering working outside of the home, even just part-time, I would recommend that you choose a job you really enjoy, and one that works around you and your family. If you hate your job, it can affect your behavior at home. And if it infringes on your family time, you will resent working outside of the home.

ALL MATERIALS COPYRIGHT ©2011 AMBER N. CARTER

Tailoring Your Business Around Your Family's Schedule

I have found that, in order for a SAHM (Stay-At-Home Mom) to be successful in her business, it is absolutely crucial that the time investment in the business be completely based around her family's schedule. In fact, the biggest challenge I face is effectively balancing my time when my work schedule demands more time than my family time allows.

I recently attended a MOB (Mom-Owned Business) Conference, which included about 60 other moms who owned and operated various types of businesses. Some moms had young children at home full time while others had children in college. Obviously, their schedule considerations differed quite a bit. With that in mind, take an honest look at your own family situation. Here are some suggestions of types of business that may work for you depending on your individual situation.

Do you have multiple children who all nap at separate times? If you need to work sporadic hours, these types of business models would work best for you:

- Service-based business with long-term deadlines (as opposed to being required to respond to urgent requests immediately)
- Distribution of an existing product on a commission basis (ex: Mary Kay, Moby Wraps, Strider Bikes etc.)
- Affiliate Marketing (earn a commission by selling someone else's product; this is commonly practiced by placing "buttons" on websites/blogs)
- Maintain a popular blog (your paycheck comes from advertisements). Warning – this isn't a huge money-maker, at least until your blog actually becomes popular.

Do your kids go to school for a part of the day? Or do you only have one child who always naps at the same time each day? If you can create some sort of office hours, these options might work for you:

- Management of service-based business (similar to my business - Carter Billing Services, LLC)
- Management of product-based business (see interview below with Melissa Berry of Missionary Chocolates for a fantastic example)
- Any of the above mentioned opportunities

Does your husband (or family member or friend) have flexible work hours, which could allow you to very occasionally leave for a longer amount of time? For instance, if you could earn $10,000 in three days, could your husband take a couple of vacation days to stay at home with your kids while you flew across the country for a keynote presentation?

- Freelance Consulting (marketing, strategy, technology etc.)
- Expert in any particular field (do you have previous work experience that would qualify you as an expert in a specific area?)

Existing Business Models vs. Creating Your Own Business

Existing Product Sales & Existing Service-Based Opportunities

If starting up a new business isn't really your thing, one option to consider could be telework for an already established company. This involves working for a company (usually as an employee) from home. If you were looking for a telework position, a good place to start would be at a current or past employer. You could also just apply to a well-known company in your industry – even if they're not posting any new positions. You may just get the job if you're perfectly qualified. Many companies offer telework positions online, however, I would caution you when applying for these types of positions – there are many online scams out there. If it sounds too good to be true, it probably is.

If you're a particularly good salesperson or have a popular blog that generates many hits, you could consider developing affiliate relationships with other companies. This works especially well if you have a personal relationship or experience with a particular product. I personally have an affiliate relationship with the *Free Agent Formula*, the entrepreneurial curriculum that I've referred to within this guide. Because I have personally experienced the program and have a friendship with the co-authors, I'm professionally well placed for this opportunity. Not only am I truly confident about this product, but also it's easy to sell – practically speaking. I just have a link on my website that refers my viewers to the *Free Agent Formula* website. If someone purchases their product after clicking on my link, I receive a small percentage of the sales. This isn't a huge money-maker, by any means, but I would recommend developing affiliate relationships with products that you could honestly endorse and just consider it a minimal, supplemental income. If you're not sure where to start, try visiting the website of a well-known online shopping cart provider and search for all of their available affiliate programs. (My favorite shopping cart is e-Junkie – check out this link for their list of programs: http://www.e-junkie.com/shop?section=affiliates).

Another option would be to buy into a franchise. One caution that I would give, if you were considering a franchise, would be to make sure you weigh the pros and cons. Yes, you may not have to worry about advertising and attracting clients, however, start up costs are usually high, you'll have to follow someone else's rules, and if another franchise owner makes a

SECTION 3 – Business Models

mistake, it could hurt your sales and reputation. One bad apple can ruin the whole batch.

If you'd prefer to become an independent contractor (as opposed to an employee or franchise owner, as previously mentioned) for an already established, successful business, here are some examples of businesses you could consider. For the most part, they fall into two categories – Existing Product Sales or Existing Service-Based Opportunities. Although there are a vast array of home-based business opportunities, the initial investment, time requirement, and pay varies quite a bit. Make sure you research your options well before you make your decision.

1. Examples of Existing Product Sales (Either Franchise or Independent Contractor)
   a. Avon (www.avon.com)
   b. Mary Kay (www.marykay.com)
   c. Moby Wraps (www.mobywrap.com)
   d. Tupperware (http://order.tupperware.com/coe/app/home)
   e. Pampered Chef (www.pamperedchef.com)
   f. Uppercase Living (www.uppercaseliving.com/)
   g. PartyLite (www.partylite.com/en-us/Default.aspx)
   h. Scentsy (www.getascent.com/join)
   i. Strider Bikes (http://www.stridersports.com/business-opportunities/)

2. Examples of Existing Service-Based Opportunities
   a. Existing Franchises (Example: Stroller Strides. www.strollerstrides.com)
   b. Become an online tutor (www.tutor.com)
   c. Independent Contractor Specific to a Particular Industry
      i. Editor
      ii. Writer
      iii. Consultant
      iv. Auditor

Creating Your Own Business

1. Create a Product
   a. Moms have a knack for creating practical solutions for other moms. This could be anything from baby products to a minivan

organizer.
b. Specialty items that reach a particular market (Example: vegan truffles)

2. Bill for a personalized service
   a. Special Events
      i. Photographer
      ii. Caterer
      iii. Florist
      iv. Children's Party Coordinator
      v. Entertainer
   b. Business to Business
      i. Bookkeeper/Accountant
      ii. Computer Consultant or Repair Person
      iii. Executive Recruiter
      iv. Marketing/Public Relations (PR) Specialist
      v. Web Site Design & Hosting Professional
   c. Family Services
      i. Baby Proofer
      ii. Etiquette Trainer
      iii. Tutor
      iv. Dance Instructor
      v. Home Day Care Provider
   d. Personal Services
      i. Art Framer
      ii. Interior designer
      iii. Housecleaner
      iv. Cooking Instructor
      v. Travel Agent
      vi. Estate Sale Organizer

Money-saving tip:
Some local news stations (ex: KATU news in Portland, OR) are constantly looking for news. They'll even tweet messages on Twitter like, "any businesses out there... (Insert scenario here)?" Make sure to follow their Twitter accounts & just respond to them. Remember to be flexible with their timelines & you'll get yourself some free advertising on TV!

3. Combine Products and Sales (Best Money-Making Opportunity!)
   a. Can your service-based business generate a product that could be sold separately? (Ex: a photographer may charge for a sitting fee, but also charge separately for the pictures)

b. Can your product-based business generate a service that could be sold separately? (Ex: if you sell a "How to Redecorate Your Living Room with Less than $100" e-book, why not offer an individualized consultation for an additional fee? Be creative- this doesn't have to be done in person. Think laptop with a live video feed...)

Time Management

We all know that we can't create more hours in the day (how many times have you heard that one?), but one thing we can control is how we spend those precious, limited hours. Am I spending my time in the most efficient way possible? The first step to becoming as efficient as possible is identifying time wasters. Here are some common ways to waste time:

- Procrastination (watch out – this one comes in various forms)
- Disorganization
- Indecision
- Unclear communication
- Completing tasks that could have been delegated
- Lack of planning
- Fatigue and/or stress
- Telephone interruptions
- Inadequate technical knowledge
- Inability to say "no"

After you've identified your personal challenges, develop creative ways to tackle the problem. For example, if you commonly find yourself answering personal phone calls during your designated office hours (resulting in no work completed and a frustrated attitude) you may want to just inform your friends which hours you are available (and unavailable) to chat.

Avoid In-Person Meetings. On a practical level, a simple way to save time is to avoid in-person meetings. Personally, for business communication, I try e-mail first and the phone second because that's most efficient for me. Don't get me wrong, I'm a very social person and love spending time with others, I just know that I'll get the job done quicker if I simply ask my question via e-mail and receive a quick response. If I find a babysitter, drop off my daughter, and drive across town just to ask the same question, I've wasted valuable time. In those few hours, I could have billed for 2 hours of my time, thrown dinner in the crockpot and maybe even ran a couple loads of laundry.

Multi-task. That brings me to the next time saving tip: multi-tasking. I'm convinced that the art of multi-tasking is perfected in the life of a mom. Caring for children and the home is a full-time job. If you're considering adding a business into the equation, multi-tasking is absolutely key. Every morning, I unload the dishwasher, start a load of laundry and quickly check my work e-mail before I start making breakfast with Jada. When she goes down for her nap, I switch the laundry, throw her toys in the toy box and start dinner before sitting at my desk to tackle my work. If my dishwasher, crockpot, baby monitor and washing machine are all running while I'm responding to phone calls and e-mails, I can be pretty sure that everything's taken care of. Do whatever works best for you in your home.

Menu Plan. Schedule your meals in advance (I personally prefer two weeks in advance – any longer and my produce goes bad). Write your scheduled meals on the calendar (or input into your PDF), write out a grocery list and only go shopping once. Every night, look at the next day's schedule and factor in when exactly you'll fit in making dinner. I intentionally schedule crock-pot dinners on days that I know will feel a bit overwhelming (multiple meetings, doctor's appointments, or anything that will throw off my toddler's schedule).

Schedule Down Time. A have a tendency to overbook myself. If I don't intentionally leave a few hours open every once in a while, I will quickly find myself rundown and overwhelmed. I'm always thankful for those couple of hours that I get to spend with my daughter just coloring in an Elmo coloring book instead of throwing her in the car for yet another errand.

Be Thorough the First Time. If I send an e-mail that's unclear or missing information, I'm pretty much asking to be interrupted for the rest of my day. Even if I'm in a rush, proofreading my content before I send it is always worth my time. Also, I try to make it a goal to finish a project (or at least complete a defined goal on a project) before I put it down again. If I pick up a project and just stress out about it without actually completing the work, I'm just wasting time.

Say "No". One of the most common themes discussed during my interviews with mom business owners was the importance of saying "no". When asked what advice she would give to a new mom business owner, it was almost always "learn to say 'no'". Just because something is a good way to spend time, doesn't mean that it's the best way to spend your time. Sure, you might be the best Treasurer for the PTA, but it doesn't mean that you have to agree to that position. It's okay to say "no" and allow someone else to serve as Treasurer (even if you would have done a better job!). For other tips on time management, skip ahead a few pages to the "Prioritize, Prioritize, Prioritize" tips under Section 7 - Words of Wisdom from Seasoned Mom Entrepreneurs

Speaking of Money

Tax Benefits

Did you know that when you work from home, you can legally write off a portion of your home expenses since it's also your office? For example, my home is 1400 square feet. The room that I perform my work is 120 square feet. That means that my home office is about 8.6% of my home. That means that I can write off 8.6% of my electricity, garbage, water, sewer AND mortgage interest. That's a pretty hefty chunk of change. Let me explain how that works exactly:

What does it mean to "write-off" an expense?

It doesn't mean that the expense is free. It just means that your taxable income is lower than it would be without the write-off. Say I earn $20,000 this year from my business, but I have $8,000 worth of business expenses (some of that includes my 8.6% of my utility bills and mortgage interest). That means that my net profit would be $12,000. I only have to pay taxes on the $12,000 amount - not the entire $20,000. This topic may sound complicated, but with the help of Turbo Tax or a trusted accountant, it's actually pretty straightforward. Trust me, working from home has amazing tax benefits.

Let's say I wasn't working at all. Not only would I not be generating extra income for my family, but also I would be throwing away the opportunity to write-off expenses that we have on a regular basis (like internet or electricity).

Free (or Very Inexpensive) Childcare

Although you may initially plan on working strictly when your child(ren) nap, there will probably come a time when you will think to yourself "I wish I could just work on this project for (insert desired time here) without being interrupted!" If you're like me

Time-saving tip:
Hire help – you pay taxes on your net income, not your expenses. So why not lower that taxable amount and give yourself more time by hiring someone to do the work that you're not good at?

ALL MATERIALS COPYRIGHT ©2011 AMBER N. CARTER

and are way too cheap to pay for traditional childcare, here are a couple of options.

Ask your family for help. Most grandparents would jump at the opportunity to have a special date with their precious grandbaby. Obviously, this isn't an option for everyone. Personally, my family lives out of town, so this isn't an option for me. For some, it just wouldn't work due to family dynamics.

Visit a kid-friendly coffee shop or play area that has free Wi-Fi. Obviously, if you can't give your kids your full attention, make sure that you visit somewhere safe, enclosed and supervised.

All I really need to work is my laptop, my cell phone, and an Internet connection. For only a few dollars, I can visit my favorite kid-friendly coffee shop (Munchkin Playland, Portland OR) and keep an eye on Jada while she climbs around fun, safe indoor play structures while I answer e-mails and coordinate client's schedules.

Kiddo Swap with other Stay-at-Home Moms. This is my absolute favorite option. Even if your friends don't have their own businesses, what mom wouldn't love some free time? Even just to go to the grocery store alone? When I have a big deadline coming up, I just plan ahead by calling a friend (preferably a friend who also has a big commitment coming up) and coordinating some kiddo swap times. For example, I may drop off Jada at her house for 3 hours in the morning, pick her up for lunch and naptime (total productivity time = 5 hrs!), then her little friend arrives after naptime for 3 hours while his mommy is super productive. It's a win-win situation for both mommies. I highly recommend this option.

Hire a younger babysitter to play with your child while you're at home. Although I wouldn't hire a young babysitter to watch my daughter while I'm away from home, I wouldn't mind working in a nearby room while a 12-year old family friend is reading stories to my daughter down the hallway. A younger sitter typically doesn't mind a lower wage since he/she's probably just excited to get the job and build his or her babysitting resume.

Work after bedtime. Although I would prefer to spend time with my husband after Jada goes to bed, there are some days when this is my only option. Also, my husband plays indoor soccer a couple of nights each week – it's the perfect opportunity for me to pound out some work while he's gone and Jada's asleep.

Invest in Independent Activities. If you have older children who can entertain themselves, you may want to stop by a teacher supply store to find educational activities that they can perform on their own while you work. Similar to the way a teacher lesson plans for a day at school, you can plan learning activities for your children to participate in while you work.

Get creative. Sign your child up for swimming lessons and bring your laptop so you can work in the bleachers while she splashes around while being supervised by her instructor. Better yet, sign her up with a friend and switch carpooling responsibilities with the other mom! There are ways to work around your family's schedule and squeeze in the hours. Sometimes you just have to use those crazy mommy skills to work it out.

Work with Your Kiddos. I saved this for last, because it's got to be the most ideal situation for stay-at-home mommies. Janelle, owner of Portland Strider Bikes (www.portlandstriderbikes.com), can complete almost 100% of her work with her kids. She distributes an already established, successful pre-bike for kids. She not only fulfills orders for clients on a national level, but also meets with local families at parks for demos where her two kids (ages 3½ and 18 months) serve as ideal salespeople as they ride around the park with their own Strider Bikes. Here's Janelle's story...

Janelle's Story

Virtually 100% of my work duties can be performed with my kids.

Mom to:
Riley & Dawson
Passion:
Offering Stability to Her Kids
Money-Makin' Opportunity: Authorized toddler bike distributor

I decided to start my own business because I knew that I wanted to quit my full-time job & stay home with my kids. I became an independent distributer for Strider Bikes when my son was 18 months old and I was 6 months pregnant with my daughter.

I had been a police officer for the previous 12 years, which I loved, but it isn't the most family-friendly career. I initially took 6 months off when my son was born, then returned on the field for a year before I resigned. I had some pretty crazy shifts that made child care difficult, especially since my husband is also a police officer. I also felt that it wasn't fair to my children to have both of their parents in such a dangerous job. Today, my son is 3 ½ years old and my daughter is 18 months old.

Financially, I had a bit of a cushion to work with when I started Portland Strider Bikes. I had saved up quite a bit of comp time when I was working full-time, so I actually received a paycheck until my daughter was 5 months old. This relieved some of the initial pressure of making money – at least for 5 months!

I decided to sell these bikes because of the low start up costs. Also, my risk was much lower since it was already an established, successful product. At first, my husband was nervous about my new venture because he thought that I'd have to purchase a ton of bikes that wouldn't sell and would just sit in the garage. Thankfully, that wasn't the case at all. I started off with a small inventory and they quickly sold. Generally speaking, I usually keep a pretty small inventory. I usually order

12 bikes at a time because I receive free shipping with on order of 12 or more.

Not only do I sell the product, I also offer a free service; I organize play dates at local parks. It started off as a fun idea from a customer, but has actually totally helped with sales. Many of my sales have generated from potential customers who discovered my play dates through my website. They saw that I was going to be in their area soon, so they would just show up at the park and ask to try out a bike. Most of the time, that results in a sale. In fact, a businessman from China, who frequently flies to Beaverton on business, even met up with me at a park and purchased a bike for his child back in China!

This type of a business works really well for me because I'm extroverted. I describe myself by saying that I have a Type A+ personality. I can talk to anybody. I think I come across as being personable, friendly & outgoing. I'm not a high-pressure salesperson, but I think that actually makes me more approachable. Because both of my young kids are expert Strider Bike riders, people feel like I can give them knowledgeable tips about the bike.

I love earning money and spending time with my kids at the same time. I love being the front-end sales person. I also love that virtually 100% of my work duties can be performed with my kids. Obviously, they go with me on the play dates. They also accompany me to the park to meet other parents who want to see the bike in person. My kids are actually the best salespeople. My daughter, who is only 19 months old, usually wants to ride her bike while we're at the park, which actually demonstrates to these parents just how fun and easy it is for a young toddler to ride the bike. Part of our daily routine is our trip to the UPS Store where we ship bikes. Not only do I have the opportunity to hang out with my kids all day, but I also get to write off my mileage when we run work errands or go to the park! I'm also proud to report that my gross sales this past year (which is only my second year in business and we're in the middle of a recession) were over $48,000; the best part is that most of it was earned while I was wearing my pajamas and bunny slippers!

I don't have fixed hours, but I do have to take phone calls and

ALL MATERIALS COPYRIGHT ©2011 AMBER N. CARTER

check e-mail throughout the day. I have to be completely flexible with my schedule. Usually people want a bike right away, so I commonly have to change my plans for the day. Even though I have a Type A personality and thrive on structured schedules, it's not hard for me to re-arrange my schedule because it's how I'm able to stay home with my kids and help support the family.

The biggest challenge with distributing an already established product is that my competition is growing. There was only one other distributor in Portland when I first became an independent distributor. Now there are about 4 of us, so competition is getting tighter. More and more bike stores are also picking up Strider Bikes now, which also hurts my sales. I really only think it'll be good for about another year due to those challenges. Christmas should be strong, but it will probably dry up soon after that. It'll be pretty hard to find something else as good as this.

I would advise any mom who's considering starting a business to just go for it, especially if you don't have to invest much up front. If you're interested in selling a product, you may want to consider selling something relating to pets or kids. Even during a recession when consumers are living on tight budgets, one of the last budget cuts they will make is cutting back on expenses relating to their pets or kids.

Running a business from home is rewarding and gives you the satisfaction of being at home, juggling kids, and running a business all at the same time. It's hard though – don't let anyone tell you it's easy, but it's worth it.

SECTION 5 – Speaking of Money

Retirement Funds for Stay-at-Home Moms

Just because you don't work for a company that matches your retirement
contributions, doesn't mean that you can't contribute to a retirement fund.
You actually have a couple of different options.

If you're married and your husband already contributes to a retirement
fund, you could just increase your husband's contributions. If you're
bringing home an extra $500.00 each month into your family's budget,
then you guys have some more wiggle room for him to contribute a larger
chunk into his. This is probably the easiest solution because there are no
new accounts to setup or maintain.

Another option is to open a separate account. Regardless of whether you
have employees or not, a retirement plan can offer a number of benefits. If
you do have employees, offering a retirement plan can boost your
business' profitability by attracting and retaining quality employees. In
addition, there can be significant tax advantages for both the employer
and the employee.

For the most part, employee retirement plans can be divided into two
categories:

> **Defined Contribution Plans:** A defined amount of the
> employee's paycheck (usually a specific percentage) is invested
> into an account. The employee bears the investment risk, in this
> situation.

> **Defined Benefit Plans:** This type of plan guarantees a specific
> benefit amount at retirement, which is usually based on
> employee's age, years of service, and pay. The employer bears
> the investment risk, in this situation.

Here are just a few of the common retirement plans available to self-
employed individuals:

> **Payroll Deduction IRA Plan:** This allows employees to invest a
> designated amount of each total paycheck (after taxes are taken
> out) into his or her separately maintained IRA (Individual
> Retirement Account).

SEP Plan: A simplified employee pension is a tax-deferred retirement savings plan. This is a popular choice among sole proprietors because the business can make tax-deductible employer contributions for the owner of the business.

SIMPLE IRA Plan: This plan is funded with voluntary employee contributions and mandatory employer contributions. This is a popular option because the annual allowable contribution is significantly higher compared with a traditional or Roth IRA and employer contributions are tax deductible for the employer.

SIMPLE 401(k) Plan: A popular option for sole-proprietors, this offers a tax-deferred retirement plan that is less complex and less expensive than a traditional 401(k) plan.

Keogh Plan: Also referred to as an HR-10 plan, a Keogh plan has high contribution limits, but is also known to have more administrative burdens and higher upkeep costs.

My little definitions are only the tip of the iceberg. As you can tell, there are many options available to self-employed individuals. This information is only meant for general education purposes; I would recommend meeting with a financial advisor to help determine the best financial plan for your business and family.

Money-saving tip:
Instead of printing documents (costs money for paper & ink) and filing them, use online data storage. There are many free options out there (my favorite is www. dropbox.com).

Your business can provide an awesome opportunity for you to not only contribute to your family's current expenses, but also invest in your family's financial future as well.

Insurance Options

Not everyone has the luxury of having employer-paid insurance benefits. Maybe your husband has excellent insurance benefits from his job, which covers you and your children. Maybe he doesn't. Or maybe you're a single mom. A large percentage of women who work outside of the home aren't actually working because their families need the extra income, they're working in order to provide health insurance to their families.

If you are part of that category and wish you weren't, let's look at some other options. First, some part-time jobs offer health insurance, such as certain teaching positions. In most situations, the trade off is that you might be required to pay a higher percentage of the insurance premium. You will have to factor this into your budget. Be creative. Is there a part-time position, with benefits, available on nights or weekends (or when your husband is at home) so that you can stay home with your kids during the day?

If you decide to take the plunge into starting your own business, the way that your business is set up will determine the type of insurance benefits that will be available to you. Currently, Health Insurance is a hot topic in legislation and so many changes are occurring that I won't even try to explain them because they'll be changing again soon. I would just recommend contacting a local insurance agent and ask him or her what the current options are for small business owners in regards to individual and group health insurance plans.

Money-saving tip:
Be sure to ask your local insurance agent if they offer a free consultation!

Types of Businesses (From a Legal Standpoint)

If you've decided to start up your own business (either service-based, product-based or a little of both), you'll need to decide what type of business would be the best fit. It's a good idea to contact a trusted CPA and an attorney to help you determine which would make the most sense for you both tax-wise and legally.

Let's look at the most common types of business entities. Take note that these are simplified summaries; your CPA and attorney can help explain these in more detail.

Sole Proprietor/No Entity
A sole proprietor is a single person who is engaging in business and is the sole owner. He or she may or may not have employees. In Oregon, if the owner chooses to use their personal name as the business name, then the business doesn't even have to file with the Secretary of State. All business related income and expenses are reported on the owner's individual tax return. Because the business is not legally separate from the owner, the owner's personal assets are liable to creditors.

General Partnership
Here's a common phrase heard from budding entrepreneurs – "Hey, we should start a business together!" Watch out! Just because someone is a good friend, doesn't mean they would be a good business partner. There are many legal risks to a partnership. For example, each partner is individually liable for the debts of the partnership, regardless of whether the individual partner even was aware of the debt. That's scary. Unlike a sole proprietorship, a partnership has two owners and the income and expense of a general partnership pass through to both of the partners. Because of the use of LLCS and S Corporations, General Partnerships aren't as common as they used to be.

C Corporation
A corporation is considered a separate "person" under Oregon law. As such, it has its own debts, for which the owners are usually not liable (except in limited situations). The owners (also known as shareholders) of a corporation typically elect a Board of Directors who is responsible for running the corporation. The Board of

Directors, in turn, appoints officers who are responsible for the day-to-day operations of the corporation. The corporation is governed by bylaws, which outline the rules, rights, and duties of each director and officer.

In order to form a corporation, Articles of Incorporation must be filed with the Secretary of State. There is a filing fee associated with this form along with an annual renewal fee.

S Corporation

A small corporation can elect to be an "S" corporation. The difference between a "C" corporation and an "S" corporation is how the entity is taxed. A "C" corporation files a separate tax return then when dividends are distributed to its shareholders, the shareholders are taxed on the dividends. An "S" corporation also files a separate tax return, but the gain or loss is passed through to the individual owners on a Form K-1, and the dividends are not taxed.

Limited Liability Company

A limited liability company (LLC) is a hybrid between a partnership and a corporation. An LLC can either be member-managed or manager-managed. A member-managed LLC operates more like a general partnership while the manager-managed LLC operates more like a corporation.

Either way, the profits and losses of the LLC pass through to each individual member. The LLC usually files its own tax return, but it does not pay taxes. Instead, each individual member pays the taxes on his/her share of the profit (or receives his/her share of the deduction for the loss).

To form an LLC, the Articles of Organization are filed with the Secretary of State. There is also a filing fee associated with the filing along with an annual renewal fee. An LLC is governed by an Operating Agreement.

Single Member LLC

Like its name suggests, a single member LLC is a limited liability company with only one owner. It operates the same as a multimember limited liability company, except that it's a disregarded entity for tax purposes. What is a disregarded entity? It just means that IRS doesn't consider the business to be separate from the owner for tax purposes. In their mind, you and your business are the same entity. Because the owner and the business are the same entity, no separate tax return is required for the business – the owner's tax return is good enough.

Tax Forms

If you decide to follow Janelle's path (independent distributor of an existing product), you will receive a Form 1099 at the end of the year from the company that produces your product. That form will just be included with your taxes as additional income that you earned. If you follow Kathleen's path (part-time work as an employee), you will receive a Form W-2 at the end of the year from your employer. The difference between those two situations is that Janelle is in charge of paying her own taxes while Kathleen's taxes are taken out of her paycheck for her from her employer.

If you follow my model (owning a service-based business which hires independent contractors), then you'll be in charge of filing your business taxes and your personal taxes along with creating and distributing Form 1099s to each independent contractor. Contact your accountant to make sure that you complete the required forms for your business.

Money-saving tip:
Free advertising opportunity! When pitching a story to the media, identify yourself as a local expert in a current, hot national topic (ex: during a bad economy - "I received 300 applications for my open position, but was only able to hire 3 people").

Words of Wisdom From Seasoned Mom Entrepreneurs

Work in an Organized Environment

- Limit your clutter.
- Have office supplies fully stocked such as scissors, binder clips, stapler, pens, highlighters, tape, paper clips, sticky notes & stamps.

Get Help

- Find a mentor or a circle of influence -people that you can rely on for help, advice & support.
- Take advantage of Mercy Corps NW; they offer a Business Planning class for new owners.
- Build a network before you need it. If someone offers to watch your kid sometime, write that down! You might need to take them up on the offer in the future!

Don't Sweat the Small Stuff

- The details of your business are like the details of a wedding - nobody knows what you didn't do. They don't know that you didn't order those Jordan almonds or embroider the napkins.

Prioritize, Prioritize, Prioritize!

- Learn to cut something off if it's not working.
- It's okay to let something slide - who really cares if your house is a little dusty?
- Ask kids to help with cleaning when they're old enough.
- Delegate responsibilities when things get overwhelming.
- List your monthly responsibilities on a whiteboard in your kitchen. It's good for kids to see how busy you are. Also, see how you feel when you read those items. If something makes you cringe, then maybe you should cut it.
- Find time to exercise. It wards off depression, improves blood flow to your brain (which is when you'll get your best ideas), increases energy, & relieves stress.
- Learn to say "no". This might mean that you let a personal call go straight to voicemail during your office hours.
- Just because something could be considered a good

decision, doesn't mean it's the best decision.
- Set aside "Personal Hours", not just "Office Hours". Maybe that means turning off the office phone and computer from the time you pick your kids up at school until they go to bed.
- Don't treat your kids like they're less important than your business. If your kids are old enough, maybe explain to them what you're doing and how it works instead of constantly telling them "Wait a minute. Let me finish this first".
- Make sure you set aside time for your husband.
- Sit back and evaluate what you want for your life. Set your goals, then figure out what that will look like on a daily basis - are you happy with that picture? For example, if you decide to hire employees, realize that you become a manager - you're not baking pies (or whatever the profession) any more - you're managing people. Is that what you want to do?

Create Defined Goals

- Know your break-even and your fixed costs & be HONEST about them.
- When you write your goals, have someone there to witness them (so that you can hear yourself saying them - it might make yourself more clear about the goal & you will have someone who will hold you accountable)
- Monitor your sales, income, goals etc. on a daily basis
- Stay on top of trends & look at possible growth

Don't Become Complacent

- Keep nurturing current clients. Document successes then use it as examples for future clients. For example, take a screen shot of a good review or ReTweet and use it in the future as proof of your success.
- Be action oriented. Go the extra mile. You'll only get out what you're putting into the business.
- Focus on a niche market; stick with what you do best.
- Be excited about your business. People will be attracted to that.

Be Positive

- A bad economy reduces competition – a recession happens about every 25 years, so a long-term business will most likely hit one at some time. Just prepare for that & have a positive attitude.
- Use others in your same profession as a support system & collaborate – don't just view them as competition – this idea has coined the phrase "Collabatition".
- Be confident when presenting your business. If you're confident, the audience will be confident in your business.

Be Creative

- Need an office, but can't afford one? Consider office sharing – split rent with other entrepreneurs who are in the same situation. Or maybe trade services with a client who has a large conference room.

You Can Do It

- You've already proven your ability to manage a household and children. Use those multi-tasking and time management skills to manage a business.
- People will tell you you're not going to make it, but that's just because they wish they had what you have.

Resources for Mom Entrepreneurs

*Many of these small business resources are Oregon specific, but it should give you an idea of what types of services are available to small business owners. You may want to check out similar resources in your area; if you're having a hard time finding them, you could try contacting these Oregon resources to ask if they know of similar opportunities in your area.

- **SCORE** (www.scorepdx.org). Service Corps of Retired Executives. Comprised of business professionals that volunteer to help businesses succeed. They offer low-cost workshops full of practical information and free counseling. Yes, FREE counseling. So start asking and start growing.
- **Mercy Corps NW.** (www.mercycorpsnw.org). Offers classes for small business owners.
- **Question Moms** (www.questionmoms.com). Affordable market research for moms wondering if others would be interested in their product or service. Offers income opportunities for other moms to provide the results of that market research via survey responses.
- **Crave** (www.thecravecompany.com). Acknowledges, celebrates & passionately supports locally owned businesses.
- **Oregon Secretary of State, Corporation Division**. (www.filinginoregon.com) Links to business name searches, forms for filing, and business registry and renewal.
- **Small Business Administration** (www.sba.gov). Programs and services specific to small business owners.
- **Small Business Development Centers**. (www.bizcenter.org) Training and technical assistance.
- **Startup Nation** (www.startupnation.com). Offers web seminars "webinars" for small business owners.
- **Internal Revenue Service** (www.irs.gov). Tax information.
- Social Security Administration (www.socialsecurity.gov/bso). Verify employee social security numbers, submit W-2s, and find benefit information.
- **E-commerce Consulting** (www.bluedeerdesigns.com). Learn more about how to properly run a website for your business and which types of online shopping carts are best for you.
- **Angela Russell**. (www.angela-russell.com). Affordable legal consultation and representation for small business owners. She offers predictable, flat rates, which helps tremendously

with budgeting.
- **Urban Mamas.** (www.urbanmamas.com). One of the many great websites geared toward working mamas.
- **Your local library.** May offer services for small business or at the very least, a variety of reference material for research.
- **Your local bank or credit union.** May also offer special services or loans to local small business owners.

For a more extensive list of over 300 resources, check out the Resource Guide from the *Free Agent Formula*, or the electronic version which is found at www.freeagentsmartsolutions.com.

Disclaimer: All of the information from this guide is from sources believed to be reliable, but accuracy and completeness cannot be guaranteed. While the author has been diligent in attempting to provide accurate information, the accuracy of the information cannot be guaranteed. Laws and regulations change frequently, and are subject to differing legal interpretations. Accordingly, the author shall not be liable for any loss or damage caused, or alleged to have been caused, by the use or reliance upon this product.

ALL MATERIALS COPYRIGHT ©2011 AMBER N. CARTER

Wife to Gabe and mother to Jada & Micah, Amber owns and manages Carter Billing Services, LLC from her home outside of Portland, OR. She is passionate about living the life God has called her to live – to serve others, raise her kids and strive to inspire and encourage other mommies. She loves speaking, writing, and consulting with small business owners about how to make the most of their business opportunities.

Share Your Story!

I'd love to hear from you! For an opportunity to be featured in a future edition, tell me how you earn money from home. Feel free to include any sort of money-saving tips, while you're at it!

carter.billing@gmail.com
www.carterbillingservices.com

ALL MATERIALS COPYRIGHT ©2011 AMBER N. CARTER

Layout and design by Clark & Co. (www.clark-and-co.com)

www.ingramcontent.com/pod-product-compliance
Lightning Source LLC
Chambersburg PA
CBHW051243170526
45165CB00004B/1561